# How to Empty tl

GW00507861

The other six titles published by F

**How to Escape from Cloud Cuckoo Land**
**Behavioural Coaching 2nd edition**
**Behavioural Safety for Leaders**
**Notes on Behavioural Management Techniques 3rd edition**
**Ideas for Wimps**
**The Too Busy Trap**

I would like to thank the following people who helped in the production of the first edition with encouragement, ideas, written text and great feedback: Nicole, John, Mat, David, Rachel, Jean, Nora, Joanne, Allison, Bob and Bruce. Thanks to Jean for the lion.

Many thanks to all the people who have completed our courses and provided us with their insightful feedback as part of their coursework. Many of the suggestions for change have been incorporated in this second edition. Finally, my appreciation to Lynn Dunlop for becoming our editor in chief and doing such a skilful, comprehensive and ruthless job.

Hollin books
21 Ashbrook Rd
Bollington
Macclesfield
Cheshire
SK10 5LF
Hlees@hollinconsulting.co.uk
www.bmtfed.com

First published by Hollin books October 2009
Second edition published August 2012
Hollin books is a division of Hollin Consulting Ltd
© Copyright 2009 Hollin Consulting Ltd

Graphics by Creative Hero
Printed in England
ISBN 978-0-9563114-4-3

# Foreword to the second edition
## John Austin, PhD

When Howard asked me to write the foreword to this book I was honoured to do so. I have been working with Howard since 2005 and in that time he's had an incredibly positive impact on my thinking and behaviour.

The content of the book, while directed at some specific problems that one might encounter at work, is much broader in its relevance than it might seem at first glance. The reason for this breadth of application is that Howard writes from a position of mastery of the behavioural science concepts that underlie each of these problems.

Throughout my career, my mission has been to translate Behavioural Science into terms that non-psychologists can understand and use in their everyday lives. I was a Professor in Applied Behavioural Science from 1996-2011. During this time I published over 100 scholarly articles and my students and I delivered over 250 papers at national and international conferences. I edited one of the largest Journals in the field of behavioural science and ran an international professional association.

I feel that Howard's behavioural analyses are, from a scientific standpoint, "spot-on."

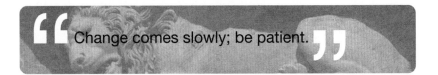

" Change comes slowly; be patient. "

The beauty of his no-nonsense style is that he cuts through all of the theory (mostly stuff you don't really *need to know*, anyway) to explain in behavioural science terms why particular behaviours are happening, and not others. He shows how, by bringing the science to life and harnessing its power, you can begin to solve your most persistent problems.

As you read, my advice to you is this:-

- Change comes slowly; be patient. Get comfortable with taking small steps. All of the world's experts in behaviour and business agree that greatness is built only through repeatedly and persistently doing the right things each day. It's simple, but by no means is it easy.
- Recognize that, although there are 80 years of research on behavioural science, you only need to know a small set of very simple concepts to start to make a change.
- Howard is a very funny guy. His sense of humour is all over this book and many of the examples are caricatures, not to be taken too literally.

There is such brilliance among the tips in this book that I urge you to plan to read it several times. Keep it as a resource and refer back to it, because I believe that over time you will see more and more that is of value to you in its pages.

The concepts described truly can be used at home, work, for the kids' football team, and in all of your relationships – should you choose to master them yourself.

To get started, find one or two people who you like talking to, and introduce them to some of these concepts. Even though it is short, this book contains enough ideas to keep you busy for years. Try some things out, have fun with your successes. Have fun with your failures. Laugh a lot. Learn through doing.

**John Austin, PhD**
Reaching Results
Portage, MI

# Contents

# 1. Introduction

Many of us spend a large percentage of our working life dealing with stressful situations which have no bearing on the job we are paid to do. After all, most of what we do at work, be it report-writing, engineering, accounting, or designing a new logo, isn't inherently stressful – it's throwing other people into the equation which causes problems!

The 'too hard' box can be described as a place to put the things we don't know how to fix, or are scared to fix. If you are one of those people who thrive on stress, then this booklet probably isn't for you. I coach a few clients who say, "Oh, it's so stressful at the moment, things are crazy," and when asked, "So, are you unhappy?" the reply is often, "No, I'm having a great time!" But for those who do have people-based problems and would like to resolve them in order to reduce stress, increase a team's productivity, make work more fun, improve home life, or even help their kids' football team win a game or two, this booklet is for you.

The aim of this booklet is to provide you with some simple things you can try out at work and at home in order to reduce the number of frustrations in your life, improve your effectiveness and hopefully make your days more fun.

At a very basic level there are two different types of 'too hard' situations:-

1. Something you need to do that involves no-one else.
2. Something you need to do which involves another person.
Obviously, type 1 should be much easier to fix than type 2. Most of this booklet will concentrate on type 2.

We spend our time on all kinds of activities, some necessary and others simply to fill the time so we have no time left to do what we know needs doing. The term for people doing anything other than the matter at hand is called 'avoidance behaviour'; it's very commonplace in the home and at work. I call this the 'too hard' box.

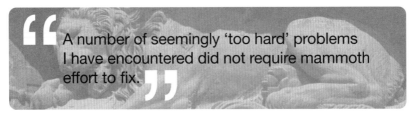

> A number of seemingly 'too hard' problems I have encountered did not require mammoth effort to fix.

I asked people to suggest what the 'too hard' box might contain and here are some of the suggestions I received:-

1.  I agree objectives with him and two weeks later he tells me why he has had no time to achieve any of them. I want to slap him. He simply won't listen to me; he doesn't want to do what I want him to do. I am at my wits' end; I can't fire him, the company won't let me.
2.  I really struggle getting past, "Look I want this by Thursday, just do it, you lazy sod."
3.  If I can do the job myself it's less hassle than asking someone else to do it, even if it's their job really.
4.  Fire-fighting is the only thing they love you for here; if you were calm and organised you wouldn't get a pay rise.
5.  How do I set clear expectations without micromanaging?
6.  How do you raise performance while cutting costs?
7.  I want to be successful in my career; I also want to have a happy family life.
8.  We keep getting it wrong on site, trying to prioritise 'safety over production'; it keeps ending up as 'production over safety'.
9.  Our lessons-learnt system has never worked; why not?
10. This place is run by finance and HR. It's pointless getting excited about anything new; they are just going to block it.
11. Why should I be the one who looks over the parapet? The bad guys need the shooting practice; I'm not going to be the target for it.
12. I need my job to pay my mortgage; there's no way I am going to risk losing it over this small problem with my boss, and I'd rather live with it.
13. I would rather do the housework than talk about my list of gripes with my boss.

14. I've been really unlucky with bosses; almost everything outside what he wants is in the 'too hard' box.
15. I don't know where I would start in trying to reduce the amount of pointless reporting in this place.
16. How can you get someone to do something in a weak bureaucracy?
17. Around here we never stop long enough to get the daily stuff right, let alone do any strategy going forward.
18. How can I overcome my overwhelming fear of failure?
19. Why would they ever give anything important to someone like me?
20. It's a complete fluke that I got this job; I'm not going to spoil things by doing something brave.
21. Is it too hard, or is it just that I can't be arsed?
22. To be honest, I find it really difficult to take my work seriously.
23. I won't do what they want here; I prefer making mischief.
24. This is all getting too much for me.
25. I thought this was a good idea but I'm finding it too hard.
26. I'm too busy right now; things here are mad.
27. My directors got where they are by being brave and assertive. I am going to try a more passive, less stressful strategy.

I think you will agree this is an eclectic list. The 'too hard' box is full of seemingly unfixable problems. There were many more, but I have tried to produce a representative sample.

Some of the 'too hard' problems look up the organisational hierarchy and some down, some with peers, some indicate helplessness and others frustration. I will categorise these 'too hard' problems and provide some strategies you could use in the chapters of this booklet.

A number of seemingly 'too hard' problems I have encountered did not require mammoth effort to fix. Factors were often at play in the home or workplace environment which distracted attention from the root of the problem. Seeing past the distractions meant that solving the problem was straightforward.

When problems actually do get resolved there are good and bad outcomes. Here are some examples:-

| Good outcomes | Bad outcomes |
| --- | --- |
| Staff member didn't realise what the boss wanted and on realisation they delivered it. | Staff member resigned at the very thought of having to do what the boss wanted. |
| The boss was simply unaware of his bad behaviour and changed it overnight. | Staff member finally told their boss why they were unhappy and got sacked for it. |

These are only extremes of some of the potential outcomes. There are things we can do to predict the outcome of a fix, and these will be dealt with in this booklet.

Behavioural aspects are normally at the heart of 'too hard' problems. Something perhaps happened to you in the past which means you now don't face up to similar situations. Observing this is one thing; doing something about it is something else.

This booklet will help you pinpoint the causes of problems and suggests strategies to help you stop avoiding the issues and start to remove the frustrations in your life.

# 2. Behavioural Science Terms Used in this Booklet

Behaviour is what people do and say; yes, it's as simple as that.

Behavioural science is the science of human behaviour; it is founded on using data and analysis to come to conclusions about what is happening with the interactions between people. Objectivity is at the core of behavioural science. Behavioural Management Techniques (BMT) is a blend of behavioural science tools and project management skills.

I have written a booklet called 'Notes on Behavioural Management Techniques' which covers behavioural terms and offers more explanation than is covered here. This chapter should be enough to help you with the terms I mention in this booklet.

Behavioural Science observes the behaviour, seeks to modify the external environment, which is the only thing we really have influence over anyway, and in doing so achieve behaviour change. Behavioural Science sees each person as an individual who desires a totally unique set of reinforcers from their environment (their world). Psychology seeks to understand what is going on inside the mind, to modify these internal phenomena and in doing so achieve behaviour change.

Both mainstream psychology and behavioural science are used in seeking to change behaviour. Critically, behavioural science has a greater verifiable record of achieving this and is also far easier for people to learn and apply.

> " Behaviour is what people do and say; yes, it's as simple as that. "

A number of scientific terms are used in this booklet. I've described these here: -

## Antecedents

An antecedent is a request or prompt, something which is attempting to drive a particular behaviour. A sign that says 'don't smoke', a speed sign, or a plan detailing how you will deliver a project are all antecedents. We are all regularly bombarded with antecedents.

Some antecedents deliver the behaviour that is intended and some are less successful. I care about the weather forecast the day before I'm going on a long walk. I care about the flight information board when I'm flying somewhere. I check what day I have to put the bins out. I look at the fuel gauge in my car when driving. Unfortunately, many work-based antecedents do not have the desired effect. Antecedents are quite poor at driving behaviour if they are not paired with consequences. Procedures, safety rules, notice boards, minutes of meetings, and requests by email will all work in part but will only work well if consequences reinforce them. If I put the bin out on Monday night it will get emptied Tuesday morning.

## Consequences

The impact of consequences is the primary effect on our behaviour. What happens to us following our behaviour will affect the likelihood of us performing the same behaviour again under similar circumstances.

Behavioural science states that there are two main consequence types that result in a behaviour occurring/recurring or stopping; 'reinforcement' and 'punishment'.

## Extinction

Extinction is the process of being ignored and can be very painful if you are the recipient of it. It is also a useful tool to use if you wish someone's irritating behaviour to go away. A subset of extinction is the extinction burst, an emotional outburst of some kind (usually verbal). This usually occurs when the behaviour is receding and is a good indicator that it is doing so.

## Environment

The definition of environment here is the immediate location of the person, be it in their office, living room, their car, wherever the behaviour is occurring. A person's behaviour is mostly driven by the consequences that follow the behaviour. The environment will dictate the consequences you experience and this, of course, includes the other people in the room, office etc. Small changes in environment can result in significant changes in the behaviour of an individual. The environment affects us and we affect the environment.

For example, imagine an office full of people. Take one person out of the office and replace them with a different person: The environment has changed. The change could be very significant depending on who left and who came in.

## Pinpointing

Pinpointing is the process used to make sure that a behaviour is described accurately. Something is pinpointed when it complies with the following rules:-

1. It can be seen or heard.
2. It can be measured, counted etc.
3. Two people would always agree whether the behaviour occurred or not.
4. It is active (something is occurring that we can observe).

People who learn pinpointing can quickly develop skills which reduce the number of assumptions in their environment. This reduction of assumptions increases the amount of informed comment, decisions and discussions.

It is advisable to gather data on situations via observations and keep notes of who actually said/did what. This significantly reduces the chance of unnecessary conflict created by assumption.

Pinpointing is a very useful skill for business. Next time someone relates something to you, if you are unsure of the message you can say, "Can you pinpoint that for me, please?"

## Shaping

Shaping is a simple concept which is very difficult to master. It recognises that you can't get from step 1 to step 10 in one vertical stride. You sometimes have to first write out steps 2 through 9 and then carry them all out, one step at a time.

People sometimes tell me, "I want to say this to my boss." Before you say anything you need to predict the chances of it being received the right way by your boss. "Not very good," will often be the reply. In these cases, you have to 'shape' to the goal you want to achieve, and this usually means a time-consuming set of steps which will shape the environment so that you can actually say what you want to say and have it produce the desired effect.

Shaping is not for the impatient, and a realisation that patience is the key can take time for some people. Many very reinforcing tools we use these days, such as email, do not help us forge a patient approach. It is reinforcing to work through a list of tasks, ticking actions off as you go. It is not naturally reinforcing to take the extra time to consider: "Is this the right thing to say? Does something else have to be achieved before I can say this and get what I want?"

Shaping is inherent in everything we learn. If you want to play an instrument, you repeat and repeat until you can play the tune. Anything that requires mastery requires repetition. Putting a group of employees to work effectively and safely requires a leader to choose carefully who will work with whom. It requires trial and error to find the best combinations. Iteration is trying things out and seeing what the result is, adjusting and trying again – this is shaping. It works; it's the only thing that does work when building a team. This is how you succeed at getting all the right people on the bus, sat in the right seats.

# 3. They Simply Won't Do What I Want Them to Do

When you ask and ask, but can't get something done, there can be a number of possible reasons for it. I'll explore a few of them here, and suggest some strategies to help you get what you ask for.

This problem applies to people who work with you, your peers, your children, partner, neighbours, etc. Here are two examples from the list in the introduction:-

- I agree objectives with him and 2 weeks later he tells me why he has had no time to achieve any of them. I want to slap him. He simply won't listen to me; he doesn't want to do what I want him to do. I am at my wits' end; I can't fire him, the company won't let me.
- I really struggle getting past, "Look I want this by Thursday, just do it, you lazy sod."

The initial questions I would ask are:-
- Do you have a relationship with the person?
- Do you have their attention?
- Do they understand what you want?
- Are they competent to do the task?
- Would they say anything to you if they didn't really understand what you want?

If your answers to the questions above are 'yes', you probably have a robust enough relationship with this person to discuss what it is that you want to happen.

A proven and well-researched process designed to achieve high motivation is to:-

1. Set clear expectations.
2. Measure performance.
3. Feedback on performance.
4. Provide appropriate consequences.

Setting clear expectations will work, providing the right environment exists for it to work. If your relationship with someone is not correct, then the chances of them doing what you want are much lower. In such cases, consider these questions:-

- Does this person ever do what you want them to do? If so, how often?
- Do they work for you; can you deliver consequences to him/her?
- Do they have a history of non-performance?
- Do they do what you want the first time, every time?

Before this person is going to do what you want every time, you will need to adjust the workplace environment to facilitate that. A good technique is to ask them to do some quick and simple things for you; easily deliverable tasks that you can slowly ramp up into more difficult ones. This will tell you if the problem is in the way you are delivering the message, or is a more complex relational problem.

There are some rules which apply to asking someone to do something:-

- Make sure you have their attention when you ask.
- Make sure there are no other distractions at the time you ask.
- Check that they agree they can do the task.
- Check that they agree with the timescale.

There is a great book called *Why Employees Don't Do What They're Supposed To Do...* by Ferdinand Fournies. It lists 16 common reasons for tasks not being completed. The overriding factor is that, when asked, 50% of employees don't actually know what they are supposed to be doing! This demonstrates that there is a problem with the setting of clearly-understood expectations.

> " Neither person wants to be the first to pop the bubble created by an unwillingness to talk honestly. "

We recently carried out a survey in a large organisation where 80% of those polled said that their biggest problem was that they did not sit down with their boss and agree what was required of them. 65% of bosses stated that they did not have time to sit with their workers and agree priorities.

It is quite conceivable that the boss is 'simmering' wondering why their direct report is not doing what they want and the direct report is sitting there wondering what they are supposed to be doing.

I have been told of this type of 'communication standoff' many times in my coaching sessions. Neither person wants to be the first to pop the bubble created by an unwillingness to talk honestly. We (humans) avoid confrontation. Even if we think there is only a 5% chance of any confrontation we will avoid the action; it's the greatest blockage to the effective delivery of feedback both up and down organisations.

It could be simple; someone could just say "Can we talk?"

Here are some things you could say in order to set up a way forward.

- "I want to see if we can improve our working relationship, it's important to me."
- "Could we talk in a neutral place, where we will not be disturbed or interrupted?"
- "Can we have a conversation please? I want to discuss some things we may both find difficult or irritable."
- "I want to improve our working relationship because it's currently causing me some stress."

Of course it's conceivable that saying "Can we have a conversation please?" is too big a step; perhaps "Can you help me with a problem?" or "Can I ask you for some advice?" might be a more likely shaping step on the way to asking for a more meaningful chat. After all, most people find being asked for their opinion both reinforcing and flattering.

If the person says "Yes, let's meet," you will now need some content to fill the meeting. For boss/subordinate relationships here are some suggestions:-

- Explore any problems the person has: "No matter how seemingly trivial, I would like to hear about any problems you have in your job."
- Explore if there are any personality clashes blocking this person at work.
- Explore if they think they have been wronged; denied a job opportunity or perhaps a departmental move, some perceived punishment - no matter how seemingly trivial.
- Explore if they would be up for a more formal expectation-setting relationship with you.
- Explore if they would be OK reviewing their performance twice weekly.

If that doesn't work, you need to have the *frog conversation* with them:-

"No matter how many times I kiss you, you are still a frog. I think the chances of you turning into a Prince are now so slim it's not worth considering it anymore."

# 4. The Overwhelming Temptation that is Micromanagement

> **"** In the absence of proper leadership people will follow anything going and if the game is to appear energetic and intelligent, that's what people will do. **"**

This problem applies to people who can't resist doing everything themselves. They are really busy at work and their direct reports are relatively free, but probably suffer varying forms of behavioural 'extinction' (the feeling of being ignored). This problem also spreads into things like doing all the cooking for their teenage children and still washing their children's clothes when they are in their twenties.

Here are three examples from the list in the introduction:-

- If I can do the job myself it's less hassle than asking someone else to do it, even if it's their job really.
- Bottom line is that fire-fighting is the only thing they love you for here; if you were calm and organised you would not get a pay rise.
- How do I set clear expectations without micromanaging?

The command and control management style, like those Dickensian men who sat looking over their glasses at the workers, supervising every move, is not available to most managers. Most white collar workers are remote from management; they get paid for using their brains; command and control is not an option no matter how appealing it is to directly supervise what everyone does.

There are many painful moments for parents as their children grow up, when they realise they cannot now control what their children do all day, every day. They have to trust them and sometimes it's not an easy thing to come to terms with.

## An issue of trust?

Trust makes life very simple and a lack of trust makes life complicated and difficult. Micromanagement commonly comes down to a boss's lack of trust in his employees. This is a hard thing to own up to, but often the case despite people's best intentions.

Perhaps it might help to ask the following questions of yourself:-

- Is there any particular reason why I don't trust the people around me?
- Is my boss causing me anxiety which I am passing on to my staff?
- Is my mistrust directed at all of them, or just one or two?
- Does my lack of trust come over to them in some way which makes matters worse?
- Does this restrict the things people are likely to say in my presence?

Some more questions you can ask of yourself regarding delegating to others:-

- Can I force myself to wait for the deadline before I mention the task again?
- Could I reset general expectations for the team that I will not nag people for the things I asked for?
- Could I get comfortable allowing people to make mistakes on business-critical things?
- Could I get comfortable working with ambiguity and uncertainty?

The truth is that if you are not comfortable giving people the chance to get competent without constant supervision then you need to take a long hard look at your role. Perhaps you should look around for a different job which is going to let you enjoy working solo.

## An issue of incompetence?

If you feel your people/children are incompetent of performing the tasks you need them to do, a number of things come into play:-

- Did you hire incompetent people?
- Did you inherit incompetent people?
- Are your children stupid?
- What are you doing to bridge the competence gap?

Our data says that when things are not working the problem is rarely one of competence. Motivation is by far the biggest cause of breakdowns of performance, both at work and in the home. Did the leader/parent create an environment for people to succeed?

In the rare cases of genuine incompetence then training is the obvious place to look. As you can tell, I'm not easily persuaded that incompetence is rife in the workplace or in the home.

## An issue of motivation?

People can become de-motivated in many ways. There are many cause-and-effect case studies which easily explain why the workers are de-motivated and the boss is busy and frustrated. If you are the boss and you are very busy there is a good chance you will be giving off many signals for your people to stay away from you. The added danger is that 'too busy' becomes a badge of honour – people emulate their bosses' 'too busy' behaviours. 'Important' comes to mean 'busy'.

It will not usually be the boss's intention to cause stress amongst the staff, but it will be an inevitable consequence of the 'too busy' behaviours. If the 'too busy' behaviours are predicated on micromanagement then this situation will quickly roll into paralysis for this part of the business.

This particular problem is very difficult to fix. It takes mammoth effort by the 'too busy' micromanaging boss to even recognise and admit they have a problem. It takes even more effort to do something about it. I have written a book called 'The Too Busy Trap' and these matters are expanded in that publication.

There was an excellent TV series in the UK presented by Gerry Robinson. He was looking to invest money in a number of small businesses which had good products but which were not making any money. The cases included:-

- A patriarchal managing director who wanted to approve everything. The office staff were frustrated. The shop floor workers were frustrated. Marketing of the products needed attention. The business was producing a quality product but was losing money.
- A third generation Chairman of a family business was forced to hire a business expert by the bank. The Chairman and new Managing Director inevitably didn't make the effort to get on with each other. The product was high quality furniture. The business was losing money.
- A family business where the elderly dad was still running the business he started many years ago. The 35-year-old, competent son was being treated like a child by his father. Many arguments, lots of anxiety; the business was losing money.
- A patriarchal managing director of a once-thriving business still wanted to be there when every part of the manufacturing process occurred; nothing could happen without his presence. The company was losing money.

In all cases the cause of failure in each business was behavioural.

I would suggest that in situations where there is a dominant boss, perhaps an owner who has been in charge for a long time, it's very easy for everyone else to escape into what's called 'learned helplessness'.

'Learned helplessness' is a psychological condition where people have learned to behave helplessly, perhaps conditioned over a long time or following a single or multiple episodes of punishment. This behaviour can continue even after the harmful or unpleasant consequences have been removed.

I know exactly how it feels: The person who is providing this consequence to you is holding all the cards; you feel you have no choice other than to acquiesce or leave the company. This feeling is extremely de-motivating and there is a chance it will live with you for some time, even after you have left the company. If you feel like this right now then you need to find some like minded people and discuss it; two heads are better than one.

## The overly political organisation

If you are working in an organisation where politics preside over performance then there may well be some strange downstream effects on people's behaviour. Politics is all about perception and behaviours will probably lean toward a competitive presenteeism. In the absence of proper leadership people will follow anything going and if the game is to appear energetic and intelligent, that's what people will do.

Breaking out of this kind of culture and hoping to do well in this sort of company will take a mammoth effort. Even then, the odds are stacked against success because the overwhelming local environment is encouraging you to join in. Get out as fast as you can!

# 5. A Question of Balance

This chapter deals with balance. How do you ensure you manage an efficient business and also keep everyone happy in their work? How do you balance cost/quality/time elements of business? How do you ensure safety is paramount and still meet production targets? Here are some examples from our list which relate to balance:-

- How do you raise performance while cutting costs?
- I want to be successful in my career; I also want to have a happy family life.
- We keep getting it wrong on site trying to prioritise 'safety over production'; it keeps ending up 'production over safety'.
- Our lessons learnt system has never worked; why not?

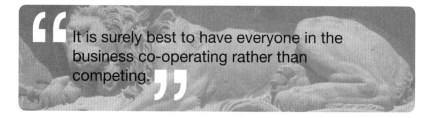

It is surely best to have everyone in the business co-operating rather than competing.

A good workplace environment is the key to efficient business. It's the leader's job to create an environment for everyone to succeed and by doing that they succeed themselves.

Setting up competing internal departments or groups in some businesses is a popular but flawed strategy. It makes no sense from a behavioural perspective. It is surely best to have everyone in the business co-operating rather than competing.

People will compete naturally anyway, without any encouragement from the company. In the summer I have the good fortune to be able to sit on the balcony of my house and write books. The house backs onto a primary school and it gets noisy at break times. If you watch the children, initially they are excited to be outside in the sun; in no time at all they are playing football, deciding who is on who's team, who is the goalkeeper etc. The same will occur at work; various power-plays will appear in the behaviour of the people in the workplace. This is natural law; it's going to happen, expect it to happen, don't get upset when it does.

The best way to approach 'getting the balance right' is to involve the performers when it comes to deciding cost/quality/time issues. It's also crucial to ask the performers of the tasks to set the measures for performance.

Ricardo Semler is the boss of Semco; he wrote a great book in 1993 called *Maverick*. Ricardo is not a trained behavioural scientist but his methods are extremely behavioural. The workplace consequences for the performers in his various businesses are directly aligned to cost/quality/time. Each work unit bids for external work and when they win work they deliver the product on time to the desired quality and within the quoted cost. This high level of involvement in all aspects of performance by the actual performers is hugely successful both for the owners and the workers at Semco.

Ricardo Semler embarked on his new work practices after he suffered ill health when he was in his mid twenties. This new style of working was his way of achieving an acceptable work/life balance for both him and his workers. Workers decide their own pay, hours of work, holidays and share of the company profits. This may sound like a bridge too far for your business but the principles can be moulded to suit any workplace, no matter how many rules you currently have in place. *Maverick* is on my all time list of 'must read' books.

I spent many years as a manager in the construction industry, and getting the balance between safety and production is perhaps more complex, as a number of competing behaviours are involved, and commonly the (lack of) time element skews priorities. Safety is a great subject to apply behavioural science to as all the consequences are literally 'life and death'.

Safety is better treated as a value rather than a competing priority. Time, cost and quality will always be competing priorities and day-to-day conversations will focus on these things naturally. Most conversations at work focus around what we did yesterday and what we will do today and tomorrow. Attempts to get people to talk about an abstract subject (safety) will inevitably fail, as topics with tangible benefits (production) will always naturally win the day.

Perhaps a better way of presenting the safety case is to review decisions. Review methods of work after the other technical considerations have been fixed and effectively give safety a veto if necessary. If everyone sees safety as a value in a plant or on a construction site then supervisors and workers will look after each other's safety. Creating a culture where people are thankful to those who are looking after their safety is the desired goal. There are many examples where companies have achieved this; these companies have little incidence of injury to their workers.

## An 'out of balance' example – Lessons learned processes

Gaining balance in business through ensuring everyone learns from past success and failure is also an honourable goal. Unfortunately 'lessons learned' processes do not have a great track record.

I worked for a company who set up a very expensive 'lessons learned' database. After 2 years' operation, and with a workforce of over 30,000 people, there were 18 lessons in the database. 'Lessons learned' processes tend to be unsuccessful for the following behavioural reasons:-

- When you are learning the lesson, everyone important knows about it anyway. Why bother to write it down in a remote database somewhere that you have never used?
- After the job is finished and it was a hard lesson(s), the last thing you want to do is write about it; you want to get out, fast.

- If you are working in a complex industry you are likely to see yourself as an expert; you are unlikely at any time to want to refer to a database full of information which would take time to search.
- Your experience with databases of this kind is not great, and you are sceptical about others' lessons - you are the expert.

You can see that there are really no reinforcers for using a 'lessons learned' database; all the consequences are punishing.

Gaining balance in the workplace is a matter of creating the right environment for your seemingly competing elements (efficiency vs work/life balance, productivity vs quality and safety vs everything else) to work towards the same ends. Creating workplace processes with reinforcers, and punishers for non-use, will ultimately lead to the equilibrium you are seeking.

# 6. This is Just the Way Things Are Around Here

There are a number of things in the 'too hard' box which could be put down to inevitability. I have separated them out as I think there are some distinctions worth discussing. Here are the comments submitted:-

- This place is run by finance and HR. It's pointless getting excited about anything; they are going to block it.
- Why should I be the one who looks over the parapet? The bad guys need the shooting practice; I'm not going to be the target for it.
- They have had a steady stream of initiatives over the years and not one of them has had any effect on this culture.

A lot of the other 'too hard' items centre on people - me, my boss, my peer group etc. This 'too hard' item is centred on the actual or perceived workplace culture.

In Charles Handy's excellent book, *Myself and More Important Matters*, he makes a very good point about workplace culture which slowly develops in organisations and constricts initiative. As rules are applied over time, the managers end up with less and less power to make decisions or be creative in a positive manner. They are left with only the power to stop things happening. He remembered rejecting a perfectly good project because he felt that without doing that he would have done nothing that week.

If everyone in the business looks at the company rules with this amount of conviction that nothing can be done, then many stupid things will occur. In a lot of cases the people inside the business will be desensitised to the stupid stuff. An outsider can come in, observe this and be aghast at what they see. I have myself been aghast on many occasions.

There are numerous stories which demonstrate rule-governed behaviours which have gotten out of hand. Here are some examples:-

- The staff nurse who refused a very sick patient an ambulance because she had filled her quota of ambulances for that day.
- The plant operator who switched off crucial safety equipment because he was in danger of exceeding his limit on electricity use that month.
- The safety advisor who refused to let the workers finish shoring up a dangerous building because they did not apply for a permit in the first place.
- The transport fleet which became 80% un-roadworthy primarily because the daily check list, which was required for repairs to be arranged, was voluminous and dispiriting.
- The night shift on railway work which was reduced over time to only 4 hours' actual work because of increasingly bureaucratic shift handover processes.

A new recruit to a company told me what his new boss had just told him. His boss said, "These are the rules around here: Keep your head down, don't volunteer for anything and whatever you do, don't screw up." This is referred to in some circles as the 'bureaucratic oath'. It is looked at with amusement by some and is associated with a number of cultural norms which are easy to predict. An organisation is unlikely to reward performance if this oath is widespread. This organisation is likely to be overflowing with examples of good ideas which are not getting suggested.

> " Some workplace cultures can be improved by locating performers in a way which supports production. "

Looking at cause and effect, it's interesting to note that in a lot of companies the Chief Executive has an office close to the Finance Director and HR Director. This element of geography on the situation can have catastrophic effects on the business. The Operational managers of the business may have less influence with the Chief Executive simply because they are remote from the centre. Workplace environment drives behaviour and geography plays a large part in that.

Some workplace cultures can be improved by locating performers in a way which supports production. Hierarchical organisations have a tendency to arrange in silos, making it necessary for permission to proceed to go to the top of one silo and then down the next silo. The return journey takes the opposite path and this takes a good deal of time as important matters spend time in various in-trays.

In these modern times of computer technology we have no evidence that these journeys are sped up. I urge people to test to see if their emails have been opened, read, understood and acted on before they feel good about having completed an email-related action.

If some people in your company do not open, read, understand and act upon your emails then you need to stop sending them emails or ask them if they would respond. Ignoring good information on people's likely behaviour is going to lead to frustration and the development of an 'it's too hard to get stuff done around here' culture.

# 7. It's Not Me, It's My Boss

It's difficult when writing these books to avoid the dreaded boss-related 'too hard' stuff. They say that people do not leave organisations, they leave bosses. I have, in my life, suffered my fair share of incompetent, egotistical, dull, selfish, mean, useless bosses. These qualities appeared all at once in the behaviour of one of my ex-bosses; he was special! There are also some great bosses out there and they are well worth holding on to.

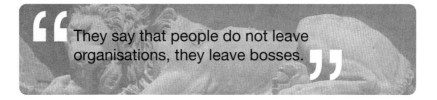

> They say that people do not leave organisations, they leave bosses.

There are many stressful situations caused by bad bosses. Here are some of the boss-related 'too hard' comments:-

- I need my job to pay my mortgage; there's no way I am going to risk losing it over this small problem with my boss, and I'd rather live with it.
- I would rather do the housework than talk about my list of gripes with my boss.
- I've been really unlucky with bosses; almost everything outside what my current boss wants is in the 'too hard' box.

I have advised many ways of tolerating life under the purview of bad bosses. Here are some suggestions for coping with the stereotypical 'under the thumb of the boss' situation:-

- Make notes of what he says, especially if there is swearing.
- Try to avoid his conversations with onlookers; some bosses like to dish out public teasing which can easily turn into humiliation (parents should watch out for this too).

- Find someone you can talk to about the behaviour of the boss and see if there is common ground.
- See if there are other people in the workplace suffering the same situation; share your observations.
- Try to shift this difficult environment by experimenting with different ways of responding to this boss. Make a note of what works and when.
- Seek ways to maintain your dignity. Small shaping steps can move a poor relationship a long way over time.

Someone once called me and said he was terrorised by his boss, who kept ringing him up and swearing at him. He was at his wits' end; life was very miserable. We chatted about things he could do to get out from under this boss but nothing was workable at that time.

I suggested that he could make it more tolerable if he was willing to predict what kinds of words the boss used when he called on the phone. He made a list of the swear-words his boss used and wrote them down. He then tried to predict which words would be used the next time his boss phoned. He mused, "one tw*t, five wank*rs, three toss*rs and a fu*k." He then ticked off the swear-words as the boss spoke. It didn't solve the overall problem but it made it much easier to live with.

You are naturally likely to fill your days with coping mechanisms if you are suffering a bad boss. The stress caused is probably going to have an effect on your enjoyment, production and performance. I have coached a number of people who have been in seemingly intolerable situations regarding their boss; it's quite difficult for me to understand why people endure such an awful workplace environment. The bottom line is that they would rather tolerate it than contemplate dealing with it, or leaving it.

If you are willing to have a go at doing something about your bad boss then there are a number of suggestions included in the 'Behavioural Coaching' booklet. Here is the basic process:-

*The first step is to start writing down what you find irritating or depressing about the various behaviours of your boss. A considerable amount of dissatisfaction with people is based on a small behaviour that gets blown out of all proportion by perception, gossip or the encouragement of others. It is crucial to write down actual pinpointed behaviours you have observed.*

*To make it easy you can experiment with your boss by testing to see what you can actually get him/her to do. Will they respond to a request for a meeting, will they reply to an email, will they read something you sent them? It's important to make notes so you can measure your progress (or lack of it).*

*If you are wondering where you can start this process then it's probable you can arrange a meeting in a quiet room for 10 minutes. You can say "I would like to pass something by you, could we meet for 10 minutes in a meeting room please." Assuming this is agreed, you will have reset the environment by agreeing to a small time-frame meeting in a neutral venue. The fact that this is different to the norm in your dealings with your boss is key to setting the stage for change. You need to prepare something to say, of course, and whatever it is it needs to have an outcome you can both measure.*

*(Excerpt taken from 'Behavioural Coaching' Hollin books.)*

I am aware of a number of 'bad boss' situations which had developed that ended happily. A lot of people are completely unaware of their own behaviour (try observing your own sometimes). Some people respond really positively to feedback on their own behaviour; yes, even some supposed ogres.

The main reason why boss-related feedback gets in the 'too hard' box is because people perceive bad outcomes. They may well be right. Sadly, even if there is only a 5% chance of being right about your concerns it will remain un-acted upon in the 'too hard' box.

# 8. The Culture Here is Just Barmy

This chapter is about cultures where lots of things do happen, but too many are the wrong things. There is lots of activity, but it is ineffective. These are represented by the following from our list:-

- I don't know where I would start in trying to reduce the amount of pointless reporting in this place.
- How can you get someone to do something in a weak bureaucracy?
- Around here we never stop long enough to get the daily stuff right, let alone do any strategy going forward.

A bureaucrat is someone who has an unhealthy appetite to stick to a set of rules he wrote himself. Rules exist for a reason - a whole host of reasons - mainly to satisfy a desire for nothing to go wrong in the organisation, or for no-one to get hurt. There are many bureaucratic organisations out there, some public and some private. A famous CEO, Jack Welch, talked often about driving bureaucracy out of his organisation. He said, "If you are not constantly vigilant it will reappear."

In many organisations the natural temptation is for people to create bureaucracy. I have mentioned the break-time behaviour of the children at the school behind my house. I also frequently overhear conversations as they set up their games and activities at playtime. These games are always preceded by decisions over who is in charge and what the rules are going to be; sometimes the rules are so complicated they never get to play the game before the bell goes. The parallels with the workplace are spooky.

One of the good bosses in my past was against the production of organisation charts. He would say, "They just tell people what's none of their business. I don't want anyone thinking anything on this project is none of their business; I want all of us to deliver this project, as a team."

> **Digging your way out of a happy bureaucracy can be very difficult.**

I can see why people would like clear roles and responsibilities to be set. Unfortunately most of the organisations I deal with are really complex when it comes to production or service delivery. The sentiment of the successful boss could be: "I would like to think that together we can deliver the whole job. If we have to write down every nuance, every possibility, before we act we may forget something and fail. Let's just succeed in a lean and appropriate manner."

Digging your way out of a happy bureaucracy can be very difficult; you can get as angry as you like and it's unlikely to change what happens, as most of the other people in the organisation are convinced that they are happy with the rules and seemingly wasteful activities. Like the schoolchildren, they do the same rule-setting activity every break time and rarely save enough time to play the game.

# 9. It's Me, part 1

Some people suffer from low self worth, low self esteem, a pessimistic outlook on life and various other negative states of mind. These are stereotypical descriptions of people and potentially inaccurate, but I expect you can recognise the type of person. They might say:-

- How can I overcome my overwhelming fear of failure?
- Why would they ever give anything important to someone like me?
- It's a complete fluke that I got this job; I'm not going to spoil things by doing something brave.

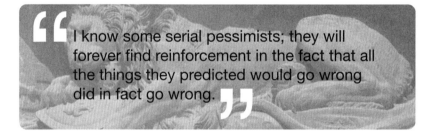

> I know some serial pessimists; they will forever find reinforcement in the fact that all the things they predicted would go wrong did in fact go wrong.

There is a massive industry out there selling all kinds of products designed to make us feel good about ourselves. I have recommended many of these books myself over the years; some are good, most are not going to produce a miracle cure. It's important to note here that there are only three things which drive behaviour:-

1. The chemicals you inherited from your parents; BF Skinner called it 'genetic endowment'.
2. All the events in your life thus far.
3. The current environment, be it your workplace or living room, including the other people in these places.

Of course nothing can be done to change numbers 1 and 2 above; recognising them, however, is important. Number 3 above is the one that can be 'operated on' in order to create change, improve things, make work more productive, make work more fun, make life more fun.

I know some serial pessimists; they will forever find reinforcement in the fact that all the things they predicted would go wrong did in fact go wrong. They would never set themselves up for anything which would have a less than 100% chance of working perfectly; this tendency leaves them with few options on their likely behaviour.

I have discovered a common dialogue amongst pessimists. I am not saying they are humourless but they will hit every suggestion, every situation, with the downside; they are the experts of downside. Unfortunately this seems to spread into their likelihood of trying out new things at work. The chances of them supporting other people's ideas are low, especially if risk is involved.

You could conclude that the antidote to the pessimist is a heavy sprinkling of optimism from a high number of optimists. However, my experience does not support this. Pessimists are reinforced by the presence of optimists; it gives them more opportunity to prove to everyone that they were right all along.

# 10. It's Me, part 2, Screw You!

This type of person is not generally unpleasant; I think the stereotypical 'natural child' fits this set of 'too hard' situations really well. This type of person seems to say: "I have to get my reinforcement from the workplace. I have decided things work best for me when I get up to mischief." Here are the quotes from our original list:-

- Is it 'too hard' or just can't be arsed?
- To be honest, I find it really difficult to take the people here seriously.
- I won't do what they want here; I prefer making mischief.
- I was very senior in my last job; being this low in the organisation is tough for me.
- My Directors got where they are by being brave and assertive, I am going to try a more passive, less stressful strategy.

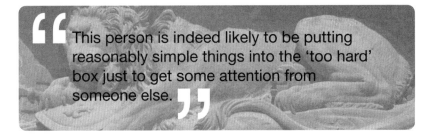

“ This person is indeed likely to be putting reasonably simple things into the 'too hard' box just to get some attention from someone else. ”

As I look over this magnificent vista, I muse over the people who fit this type. The thing I liked about Dr Eric Berne's work is the list of adjectives which describe his various 'types' of people. He likened these to 'tapes' recorded from life experiences so far, which people play back in various workplace situations. He described the 'natural child' as someone who exhibited the following characteristics:-

- Spontaneous.
- Honest.
- Genuine.
- Undiplomatic.

- Unprejudiced.
- Fun-loving.
- Jovial.

The kinds of behaviours you could expect from a person who embodies the characteristics in this list would be what we call 'attention seeking' behaviours. This person is indeed likely to be putting reasonably simple things into the 'too hard' box just to get some attention from someone else.

Engaging this person in coaching may well produce interesting conversations but also frustrating outcomes for the coach. The outcomes are different for the two protagonists. The coach wants to improve the situation, help the client etc. The person wants to use the opportunity to maximise entertainment for him and if that means downstream pain for the coach, then so be it.

Work is seen as a vehicle for the entertainment of this person; if others want to join in then great, but that's not necessary. In a lot of cases of the 'screw you' type I have found myself and members of my team in very frustrating situations as little rumours grow arms and legs and we get dragged into internal company strife as we provide the protagonist with a new vehicle for their mischief.

Eric Berne said that the only effective antidote to the behaviour of the 'natural child' is to respond in 'Adult'. In other words, stay calm, use facts, be rational, be positive, and suggest a way forward; above all don't join in with the mischief.

Some organisations have an overly healthy appetite for the use of stereotyping tools; these can have some undesirable downstream effects. They can on occasion provide people with classic lines like, "Oh yes, I'm a 'shaper'. That's why I never finish anything off." Using a given stereotype to justify unacceptable or quirky behaviours is not at all helpful in the workplace and can be quite destructive with relationships in the home.

"You'll get used to my little idiosyncrasies darling," he said, as he removed the branding iron from the fire!"

# 11. Please Don't Help Me Any More

When we carry out training courses there are a number of people who quickly see that learning behavioural science is interesting and fun. Well, it's interesting and fun in the classroom during the courses. They develop a new relationship with an intelligent and interesting trainer, and receive reinforcement from them when completing coursework. As soon as they are out of the classroom and back in the workplace, though, it can all seem much less like fun.

Because the trainer knows about 'shaping', 'stimulus control' and 'aligning consequences to results' they can usually get a large proportion of course attendees to complete their coursework right up to the last module. After the last course module is complete, things tend to fall down. Because the consequences of turning up to a course are removed from the person's environment, the reinforcers for completion of homework are no longer available to them.

Attempting to get course attendees to complete the last coursework via telephone or email is not usually successful, and we cannot expect it to be without a new set of conditions being created in their workplace. The kind of comments we get from people, post-course, can include the following:-

- I'm too busy right now, things here are mad.
- I thought this was a good idea but now I'm finding it too hard.
- This is all getting too much for me.

Feedback from post-course surveys show that people were happy with the course, they say they learnt things, that they intend to learn more about behavioural science in the future. Sometimes past course attendees keep in touch and do continue to learn more. All our trainers are past course attendees who liked the idea of teaching, me included.

> **The local workplace environment decides which behaviours will receive reinforcement and which ones receive punishment; that's natural law.**

The local consequences in the workplace environment, however, will always remain the major force in deciding who does what in that workplace. The course will probably be a remembered source of reinforcement for the past attendees and if something else similar is offered, it will probably be accepted. However, unless you continue to be reinforced for applying the knowledge and skills you gained, you will stop using them.

People who embark on post-course coaching get an opportunity to continue to deliver their improvements, test out various shaping steps, learn the tools and have someone to bounce ideas off who is expert in behavioural science: these things are all reinforcing. There are a number of people who are still very well connected to the BMT folks they met on courses. These people get regular updates of new material, the latest 'good book' to read and interesting things to view on the web. In return we get great feedback and lots of source material for our books.

The local workplace environment decides which behaviours will receive reinforcement and which ones receive punishment; that's natural law. If your environment does not reinforce you for trying to make changes then you must address this immediately, or extinction will set in and your efforts, skill and knowledge will fade away, leading to learned helplessness. Eventually you will be sat there dribbling and mumbling meaningless incoherence.

# 12. Getting Health Tips from an Old Fat Bloke?

> **"** Many behaviours are simple to observe and understand, but very hard to change. **"**

Many behaviours are simple to observe and understand, but very hard to change. The behaviours associated with a healthy lifestyle are a great example of this. Many people in the western world are overweight and lead unhealthy lifestyles. Once people have succumbed to this sneaky motivational trap it's very difficult to recover from it in a sustained way. We can easily get lots of data showing the results of what we put in our mouth on a daily basis, over a long period of time.

The convenience of take-out food and the social aspects of alcohol make it easy for us to get caught in the trap. When we are young we can eat and drink excessively and it seems to have little or no effect on our weight or health. As we grow up, perhaps we spend more time sitting in front of the TV, snacking. In the USA particularly, many 'social' foods are high in sugar and salt. All this contributes to an unhealthy lifestyle, culminating over time in the all too common heart disease and diabetes problems associated with unhealthy lifestyles.

In November 2011, I embarked on a change of lifestyle in order to lose weight, get fitter and see if I can get my blood sugars reduced from being perilously close to diabetic levels. I decided to go walking in the country around where we live as often as possible. Eat three square meals a day. Cut out snacking and only drink alcohol when on holiday, or on special occasions (Fridays and Saturdays do not constitute special occasions). I did this successfully and the data is now (July 2012) as follows:-

1. I am now out of the danger zone on blood sugars. If I still am safe in November, I will be one of the few people who leave the diabetic clinic through the right door.
2. I have lost 10kgs (22lbs). I am now 93kgs (204lbs).
3. I wear clothes two sizes smaller than when I started.
4. I can walk 5 miles at a startlingly fast pace; now no-one else wants to come walking with me.
5. I still have a way to go still to get to my target of 87kgs (190lbs), another 6kgs (14lbs) to go.

There have been a number of distractions along the way: an extended holiday for my wife's birthday; some business trips, including (and most damaging) a trip to the home of eating - those United States of America. These distractions provided me with ready excuses to eat, drink and be merry, something I am very good at. There are also threats for me in the future in the form of holidays and conferences abroad.

A common question I'm asked is, "How do you change eating habits and what does it feel like?" Well, it sounds silly, but it feels like bereavement. I like food, have liked it for a long time, and seeing food and not eating it is punishing at first. Behavioural science says that punishment is always immediate and reinforcement (especially for healthy living) can be delayed. I struggled in the early days to find any reinforcement at all. Of course once I lost some weight I was feeling much healthier. I found it very reinforcing wearing new, better-fitting clothes. Getting compliments from people, even for a fat old bloke, is nice, surprisingly nice for me. People who know me will know I am not a fashion guru!

## Finding reinforcement

I developed a technique of looking at the food I cannot eat; crumpets, sausages, bread, cakes. I visualise ordering it from the shop assistant and then decide not to order it at all. As I walk out of the shop I get my reinforcement for resisting that temptation. "I spit in the face of temptation," I say as I'm walking out of the shop (trying not to be overheard). This technique builds quite well as you get good at it;

look at all the items in the shop you can't eat, visualise buying them and eating them and then just buying what you went in for, nothing more. Walk out of the shop – collect your reinforcement (talking out loud to yourself is optional; I find it soothing).

I had to change what I ate and drank. I went from drinking wine at home to drinking fruit juice. That didn't change anything as juice is packed with sugar. I tried watered-down juice which was better, now I just drink water. Changed from semi-skimmed milk to skimmed. From bread to oatcakes. I eat more fruit. Eat muesli for breakfast. Salads for lunch, nice salads; pear & beetroot, brown rice with oily fish. We generally have meat of some kind for dinner, white meat mostly or fish. We both like cooking so we have no trouble creating lovely, healthy dishes.

## Beware the evil sales people

Supermarkets are designed by behavioural specialists to get you to buy lots of fattening crap you don't really need or want. The best way to combat this temptation is to get your main shop ordered online, using a standard list, and get it delivered to your home. That way, you are not walking past chocolate to get to the toilet rolls.

You can also leverage your own pride by telling the butcher you are on a diet and not eating bacon, black pudding, sausage etc. Tell him you will be ordering chicken fillets, oatcakes and lean pork from now on. When you succumb he will give you a knowing smile!

By using behavioural science you can design new antecedents which change the environment. This creates different outcomes that can attract new reinforcers.

## The penitent rambler

One Saturday we went to our daughter's house. I drank wine and ate too much take-out food, got drunk, then ate some more fatty crap. The next day I felt guilty, so I embarked on an extra-long walk.

Two hours of walking the hills was much harder than the eating and drinking of the day before. Doing this from time to time puts everything into perspective. I realised that it would now take me two or three days to get back on course because of this fall from the wagon. If you change the antecedents, then the consequences shift. I always discover pleasant surprises in the new consequences.

## The great by-product

I read Stephen King's book *On Writing* some time ago and found it to be interesting, useful and inspirational. He also goes walking in the hills. He said he found that it clears the mind and also gives rise to many really good story-lines. I carry a recorder with me when I am hill-walking and will commonly record 10-20 ideas every walk. My solo walks around Bollington, which I started only for the health benefits, also produce a highly creative environment for my work.

# 13. Nail the Lid Down and Throw it Into the River

While I was sending out early drafts of this booklet to the good people I mentioned at the start, I was receiving lots of feedback along the lines of: "Can you help people with ideas of what they can do if…."

Others commented that the end of some of the chapters leaves the reader wondering: "So is that it; tough luck, there is no solution?"

I have tried to give suggestions for solutions to the generic stresses people experience in their workplace. I have attempted to provide ideas of things people could say to solve their lot. The bottom line, however, is that the workplace is in perfect equilibrium right now. If anyone is going to try something new then the equilibrium will be disturbed and the resulting new environment may not be acceptable either; indeed, it could be worse.

> " The bottom line, however, is that the workplace is in perfect equilibrium right now. "

Hindsight is 20/20, I know, but recognising something is going pear-shaped, and doing something about it before it becomes a norm is the best policy. In fact, I would say it's best to be vigilant and squash anything in the environment which looks like it could make things worse. Complacency is rife in business. A lack of push-back reinforces people doing stupid things that add no value or make matters worse. Aubrey Daniels witnessed some unpleasant behaviour on a train and said to himself, "Someone should do something about that. Hang on a minute, I am someone." Once he acted, other passengers joined in to help him and the situation was resolved.

Other ways of avoiding items falling into the 'too hard' box are:-
- Don't leave things unsaid, no matter how trivial; today's minor irritation can soon turn into WW3.

- Be especially clear with people about what you want; test for knowledge. You don't have to be sarcastic; it can be done effectively.
- Make sure you are clear with your boss what he/she wants. It's worth testing any crack of uncertainty there and then. If you walk away with half a story things can only get worse.
- It's quite useful starting a sentence with "For the avoidance of doubt…" This way you can be sure you understand what's required.
- Get together with colleagues you trust and ask their advice about volatile people in the workplace; get their ideas for solutions to any potential confrontation.
- Keep people informed of progress; this avoids any extinction issues.
- Respond in a timely fashion to your emails, phone calls etc.
- Provide people with feedback on their ability to explain what they want. This will draw attention to the need for clear expectations and should be reinforcing for them.
- If you are asked by someone "Why do you want that?" or, "Why are you going there?" try saying with a smile, "What's up, don't you trust me?" This gentle push-back is quite successful in improving an intimidating environment. It only works face-to-face. It most definitely doesn't work on email.
- A lot of people will not discuss things they are worried about for fear of it appearing trivial. If you share your thoughts you will probably discover that others have the same concerns.
- If you are struggling getting someone's attention then this phrase usually works well: "Is there any reason why you wouldn't take feedback off somebody like me?" The threat is very mild.
- There is no substitution for frequently asking yourself, "Am I happy doing this job in this place?" If not, then act.

The primary reason I suggest to people, "Just try something new, anything," is that previously undiscovered-consequences can be both excellent in and of themselves, but can also uncover hidden treasures. By doing the 'right things' you will discover fortune.

Most of us don't have any problem writing down 'good leadership behaviours' and 'good parenting behaviours'. We already know what the right thing to do is. Doing it consistently, that's the goal, create the right environment for success and you will get success.

# Appendix A

## Other Hollin Books Publications

### NOTES ON BEHAVIOURAL MANAGEMENT TECHNIQUES 3rd EDITION
By Howard Lees
ISBN number 978-0-9563114-1-2
£6.50

### HOW TO ESCAPE FROM CLOUD CUCKOO LAND
By Howard Lees
ISBN number 978-0-9563114-0-5
£6.50

### IDEAS FOR WIMPS
By Howard Lees
ISBN number 978-0-9563114-6-7
£12.00

### BEHAVIOURAL COACHING 2ND EDITION
By Howard Lees
ISBN number 978-0-9563114-2-9
£6.50

### BEHAVIOURAL SAFETY FOR LEADERS
By Howard Lees and Bob Cummins
ISBN number 978-0-9563114-5-0
£8.50

### THE TOO BUSY TRAP
By Howard Lees
ISBN number 978-0-9563114-7-4
£6.50

www.hollinconsulting.co.uk